It should't happen to a

TRAINER

KAREN DAVISON

Dedication

For Ciara

Acknowledgements

I wish to thank all the dogs and owners that continue to make my life interesting, and without whom this book would not have been possible.

My sincere gratitude to Joan and Michael Downs for all their help, advice and support and my brother Andy, for his wisdom and guidance.

Appreciation to Louise Darvid for her editing skills and Elizabeth Mackey for a great cover design.

TABLE OF CONTENTS

Introduction

Have you ever wondered what ends up on the cutting room floor when watching celebrity dog trainers on the television?

During my career as a professional dog trainer and canine behaviourist, I have had the privilege of working with many wonderful dogs and good owners. It can be a rewarding job as well as a challenging one; often you have to think on your feet and you certainly can't afford to be a shrinking violet.

It is difficult to describe that sinking feeling when you hear the splash of urine a split second before the warmth soaks through your jeans, trickles down your leg and into your boot. I also have to say that my legs have seen more action from male dogs than I care to think about. I have been battered, bruised, flattened, tied up in knots and have had to deal with some situations that celebrity trainers would probably not care to admit to.

Despite all this, I wouldn't swap it for the world. Dogs are my joy in life and there is absolutely nothing else that I would rather do.

Here, I will share some of the most funny, embarrassing and surprising moments of my journey, as well as some of the frustrations, which I hope will give you some insight into a life working with dogs and their owners.

One of the most mortifying incidents involved a signpost, a middle-aged Polish gentleman and a very large dog, which turned into one of those 'you couldn't make it up' moments.

Intrigued?

Working in Ireland

I emigrated from England in 1990, setting up home in County Kerry on the southwest coast of Ireland. With its rugged mountains, lakes and the longest coastline of any county, it is renowned for its beauty. While working as a dog behaviourist, I have travelled the length and breadth of rural Kerry, much of it off the beaten track and often in reverse gear. This is usually due to obscure directions resulting in lots of three-point turn practise, or backing up to the last passing place because there is a tractor coming the other way.

Postal addresses in rural areas have no house numbers, street names or postcodes. They are simply the general area where the house is located. This means that there can be thirty properties spread over several miles with exactly the same address, which can make finding a particular house a tad challenging. Locating places can be further aggravated by vague directions; I once found myself negotiating a potholed, single track road with the instructions to take a track on the right just after the funny shaped tree. Distance perception varies enormously; 'about a mile' can be anything from a hundred yards to six miles.

Ireland has many quaint features, the sense of humour at the road signs department for example. While on main roads, signposts are on every junction, which is most helpful. Once directed off the main road however, you are led down a maze of small roads with many crossroads and junctions where signposts are conspicuous by their absence. The approach seems to be that they point you in the general direction; then you're on your own.

There are some cultural differences in the Irish approach to pets, which is somewhat more relaxed than I was accustomed to. It took me quite a while to get used to the fact that in Ireland, you see large numbers of dogs running loose all the time. Town dogs take themselves off for walks and meet up with their regular friends to find adventure, while in rural areas you often have to run the gauntlet of sheepdogs and terriers that break cover of concealment to chase your car up the road, trying to bite your tyres.

A good proportion of dogs live outdoors, which

means that much of my work is carried out in the elements. In Ireland, this can be an uncomfortable experience. Autumn is the season of constant rain and gale force winds. Winter is like the twilight zone; it never seems to reach full daylight and rains most days. Spring can see rain for weeks on end with no respite and summer can be glorious - if it is not raining.

When trudging through muddy fields in the lashing rain, it sometimes occurs that there may be easier ways to make a living. Occasionally after training I have to call into the supermarket to pick up supplies. I get many sympathetic glances from women who look like something from *Vogue* magazine with their designer clothes, perfect hair, impeccable make up and high heels. In contrast I stroll up the aisles in my walking boots caked in mud, splattered jeans, my dog training coat covered in muddy paw prints and my hair, which looked halfway decent when I left the house in the morning, plastered to my head.

Notes to self:
Should have moved to Spain.

An
Encounter with
Bruno

Caroline contacted me with an appeal for help. Bruno, her three-year-old Great Dane had turned her into a social outcast with his over-exuberant greeting behaviour. It had got to the stage where friends and family refused to visit her home.

When asked about his general behaviour, Caroline admitted that she had tried and failed in all her attempts at basic training. She had taken him to group training classes six months previously, but his uncontrollable and disruptive behaviour had caused no small amount of embarrassment, resulting in the trainer asking them to leave half an hour into the first class. Walks were non-existent, as she was unable to control him on the lead.

When asked about his diet she said that he was

getting a food designed for racing greyhounds. Apparently her husband was getting a good deal on it at the local farmers' market, to which she was adding extra tinned meat.

So just to recap, she had a giant dog that had received no training, was getting no exercise and was being given rocket fuel for food. Ho hum. It sounded like I was going to have my work cut out for me, but always up for a challenge, I made arrangements to call out to the house. It would be a few weeks before I could accommodate them, so in the interim, I advised an immediate change of diet.

I phoned the morning of our appointment to confirm directions and to ask that Caroline act as she normally would when receiving visitors. This technique allows me to assess how the owner's control of the environment and their reactions influence the dog's behaviour. Caroline informed me that the new food had already made a difference and Bruno seemed a bit calmer. Things were looking up.

Finding the house was straightforward. I turned off the road, through the stone pillars and along the gravel driveway, which led to an attractive bungalow. As I got closer, I noticed that the yellow paint was covered in muddy paw prints, some of which were higher and larger than any paw prints had a right to be. *Blimey, how big is this dog?* Greeting me at the door, Caroline gave me a

14

warm welcome and invited me in; she expressed her gratitude for my help and told me that her husband had said that I must be a very brave woman.

Bruno was secured in the kitchen at the end of the hall and as I entered the house, I could hear him barking and scratching at the door. His bark was loud and deep, you could almost feel it in your chest, all the evidence pointed to a sizable dog.

As Caroline indicated that I should enter the lounge, Bruno managed to hit the door handle and let himself out. The next few seconds seemed to happen in slow motion.

The door flew open and crashed against the wall, spraying fragments of plaster into the air. Bruno, a Great Dane the size of a small pony, shot out of the kitchen and built up surprising speed on the slippery tiled floor. Caroline threw her arms out and screamed, 'STOP, BRUNO, STOPPP.' I backed into the lounge to get out of the way as he attempted to apply the brakes. In a scene reminiscent of *Scooby Doo*, Bruno leant backwards, his eyes wide with surprise as he went into a four leg skid. At the very last moment he slew his back end sideways and hit Caroline like a bowling ball achieving a perfect strike, taking her legs out from under her.

Barely pausing to right himself, he shrugged her off and leaped in my direction. As all four feet left the ground he slammed into me, his momentum carried us both over the arm of the sofa. Ending up flat on my back on the couch with Bruno on top of me, he proceeded to smother me with slobbery, slimy kisses from a tongue that was nearly bigger than my face.

One saving grace, at least it was a soft landing. It was just as well the change of diet had made him calmer, or I might not be here to tell the tale!

Picking herself up, Caroline said, 'Now you can see why people are reluctant to call to the house.'

No sh*t, Sherlock!

Once I managed to extract myself from underneath the dog, I began to introduce Bruno to clicker training, marking his calmer behaviour with a click followed by a treat. He soon understood that calm behaviour was more rewarding and started offering it more consistently. Getting him levelled off made Bruno more receptive to learning new things. Caroline learnt how to utilise the clicker, and using this method was amazed that she was able to get Bruno to sit, hand touch and lay down on command by the end of the session. She was keen to try some new commands; leaving her with a copy of *The Perfect Companion*, which contains detailed instructions for further training, Caroline promised to put in daily practise.

When I arrived the following week, I was gratified to see Caroline and Bruno out on the lawn practising lead training and doing remarkably well; full credit to Caroline, she had obviously put a lot of work in.

One of Caroline's more courageous friends had volunteered to visit so that we could work on Bruno's greeting behaviour, and despite her friend being somewhat apprehensive, he was pleasantly surprised by the results.

It goes to show you that if you give people the right tools, miracles can happen.

I have kept in touch with Caroline, and she reports that Bruno has turned into the model dog. He is much calmer and is getting daily walks, which they both enjoy. Caroline has got her social life back and is now able to appreciate and enjoy her dog.

Lessons learnt:

My Tai chi teacher, Sensei Eamon, taught me how to sink my weight into the ground to become a strong and immovable object. Sorry Eamon, no amount of sinking of a 5'10,' 68 kilo frame, balanced on two pathetically inadequate size 7 boots, helps when you are hit by a 7'3,' 90 kilo Great Dane travelling at speed.

The Disappearing Dog

People often phone me for advice when considering a rescue dog. Although I may make loose suggestions of suitable breeds for their circumstances, I tell them that they will most likely recognise the dog that is meant for them; some things are just meant to be. This was the case for Mary and Amber.

Amber, a Springer Spaniel, was originally destined to be a working dog but it soon became apparent that she was gun-shy, so she was handed into the rescue centre for re-homing. Mary visited the centre looking for a companion dog. Despite there being many lovely dogs looking for homes, as soon as she saw Amber, she felt an instant connection with her and the decision was made.

It was a match made in heaven.

Amber was a little shy, so Mary asked me if I could help her with some basic training and general confidence building. Over the course of a few sessions, Amber responded admirably to training, her confidence was much improved and the bond that developed between herself and Mary was heart-warming. For our final lesson, we decided to have a session at Mary's local beach.

It was one of those rare dry and sunny days in early November and while there was little heat from the sun, the day was bright and clear. From the car park on the top of the cliffs, the view out across the Atlantic was spectacular. The coastline was dramatic and just off shore, rocky outcroppings protruded above the waves.

We descended down a steep winding walkway onto a sandy cove, islands of rocks worn smooth by the tide dotted the beach, which was enclosed by high cliffs. Out on a lovely day in beautiful surroundings, sea air in my nostrils and the raucous cries of sea gulls wheeling overhead, it's a dirty job but someone has to do it!

We spent an enjoyable hour working Amber on an extendable lead, going through all the training exercises and games. It was a Wednesday morning and despite the unseasonably good weather, we hardly saw a soul. I had brought along some flotation toys, and suggested letting Amber off the lead so she could enjoy some water retrieval games. She had taken to this like a duck to water, and with great enthusiasm was bounding back to us through the shallows, dripping wet, toy in her mouth, when suddenly someone let off a shotgun nearby. The blast echoed and magnified as the sound waves ricocheted around the surrounding rocks.

Amber's reaction was instant. Dropping the toy, she tucked her tail between her legs and in a flurry of sand and fur she took off as if the devil himself were at her heels. Straight as an arrow, she ran at full gallop towards the far end of the cove.

When animals suffer acute stress from fear or threat, the body undergoes a biological response known as fight or flight. This primitive instinct triggers the hypothalamus in the brain, the heart rate and blood pressure rise, muscles flood with adrenalin and glucose and the individual becomes tense and alert, instantly primed to either flee or fight. In this state it is extremely difficult to get through to them, and all our attempts to get Amber's attention fell on deaf ears.

Thinking there were no exit points other than the one leading back to the car park, I thought that Amber would be safe in the enclosed environment. However, as I watched her retreat into the distance I began to get alarmed, she wasn't slowing down despite her close proximity to the cliff face. Just as it looked as if she would run full pelt into the rocks, she suddenly veered right without breaking pace, and bounded up steep steps that I hadn't noticed at the far end of the cove. It was at this stage that I had my own biological response. Dumping my gear on the sand I took off in pursuit. I could feel adrenalin powering my limbs as I ran, trying to keep Amber in my sights. She reached the summit, and the last thing I saw was her tail disappearing over the ridge.

I was afraid that given the speed Amber was travelling I may never catch up with her, or that she may come to harm. Flying over the soft sand with a speed that I didn't know I was capable of, I covered the distance to the end of the cove. With my heart racing and arms pumping, my arthritic knees took the steep treacherous steps two at a time. On reaching the summit, I discovered another pathway leading down to a neighbouring cove. Descending as fast as I dared, I frantically scanned the distant horizon to see if I could catch sight of her. As I reached the beach, I spotted Amber behind some rocks a short distance away, just sitting there on the sand.

When I called her name she ran over wagging her tail, thankfully none the worse for wear after her ordeal. I wish I could have said the same for myself. An oxygen tent and a lie down would have been most welcome. With beads of sweat turning clammy on my skin, I bent over in an attempt to drag some air into my lungs. As the relief flooded over me, I began to shake, and my legs turned to jelly.

After taking a few moments to catch my breath and gather the strength for the return journey, I retraced my steps on wobbly legs. When we reached the pathway back to the cove, Mary was just heading up the steps, looking extremely worried and as Amber ran to her, her anxiety dissolved into a joyous reunion. I had left Mary with all the speed and grace of a gazelle; my return was more akin to a new-born foal that had yet to gain control of its legs.

Notes to self:
Expect the unexpected.

Lessons learnt:
Fight or flight response in dogs can cause even the most reliable animal to become deaf and unresponsive.
Fight or flight response in middle-aged dog trainers can cause amazing physical feats beyond their usual capabilities, leading to many days of pain and regret.

Looks Can be Deceptive

When working as a dog trainer, you have to be flexible in your approach. Not all training methods suit all dogs. Sometimes I have to develop new ways to teach a command on the spur of the moment, as the particular dog I am working with does not respond to methods that would normally be successful.

You also have to learn to be just as adaptive in your approach to owners. Being a dog trainer involves a deep understanding of dog behaviour as well as a reasonable grasp of human nature. While I like to think that I have, over the years, developed some small insight in this area, there have been instances when I have completely misread a person. Kathleen was a case in point.

Patrick contacted me to ask if I could help his

mother as she was experiencing some problems with Max, her Jack Russell. Patrick accompanied Kathleen to the appointment and when they parked outside my office, I could hear muffled frantic barking emanating from the boot. I went out to greet them just as Patrick was handing Kathleen her walking stick and helping her out of the car. He was a giant of a man and she was a small frail eighty-year-old lady, who despite the warm day, was bundled up in many layers of clothing. After introductions, Patrick suggested that Kathleen go inside while he took Max for a toilet break before joining us.

Kathleen seemed a little unsteady on her feet and walking seemed to cause her some pain. Once inside she sank gratefully into the proffered chair. While we were waiting for Patrick and Max, Kathleen and I chatted amiably. With a gentle smile, she spoke fondly of her six sons, nine grandchildren and three great-grandchildren. She obviously doted on her family and was probably the same with her dog.

The volume of barking got progressively louder as Patrick made his way in with Max. He was large for a Jack Russell, and his muscle tone was impressive. His thigh muscles were corded and stood out in clear definition as he strained against his choke chain which caused his bark to turn into a choking cough. Patrick explained that he was not used to being on a lead and hated going in the car. When we removed the chain and lead, he began pacing, jumping up at the windows and doors and barking, looking for a way out.

'He's very stressed at the moment,' I said, 'is this normal behaviour for Max?'

'He's like it all the time,' Kathleen said. 'He constantly wants to go out, and when I lets him out, he takes off over the field and won't come back. I calls him and calls him and he ignores me.'

'I see, so you haven't got a secure garden?'

'No, I lives out in the country and it is all open,' she says.

Looking at Patrick, I said that this would have to be addressed, and we discussed possible fencing solutions to make a secure area off the back door to contain Max when he was let out. He confirmed that this could be done. I also made a note to start lead and recall training. Turning back to Kathleen, I asked, 'So how do you manage to get him back?'

'I haves to chase him round and round the field!'

The idea that this frail elderly lady would be able to chase a young energetic Jack Russell around a field with any success was mind boggling. Even a tortoise would have given her a run for her money.

'How on earth have you been managing that?' I asked.

'Well, I goes over for an hour or so, then I have to go home to lie down for a bit, then I goes out and tries again. Sometimes it can be going on all day. When he gets hungry, he comes near enough for me to catch him.'

This situation needed an immediate resolution. Kathleen was in danger of doing herself a serious mischief.

'Do you give him a treat when he comes back?' I ask.

'No I don't, I gives him a good beating with my stick!'

I did a double take.

'Sorry. What?'

'Yes, I gives him a lesson he shouldn't forget,' she said.

All righty then. My impression of Kathleen in the role of the doting owner needed adjustment. This revelation certainly explained the dog's frantic escape behaviour, high stress levels and well developed muscle tone, he was terrified of her.

Kathleen seemed genuinely surprised when I pointed out that if she beat me with a stick every time I came near her, I would run away from her as well! I began to explain the benefits of reward-based training, but I could tell that Kathleen was less than impressed with the idea. She looked at me as though I had two heads.

Changing tack, I asked her if she enjoyed having Max for company.

'No, he's nothin' but a nuisance. I'd be glad to see the back of him.'

Yep, definitely misread this one. Judging by Patrick's reaction, this was news to him.

It transpires that Kathleen didn't actually want a dog in the first place. The family had clubbed together and bought Max, so that she would have some company. This well-meaning gesture was making Kathleen's life difficult and Max was paying the price. Poor dog. It was decided that it would be best for all parties if Max could be found a new home.

Getting a dog is a big decision and should not be taken lightly; it involves many years of responsibility, commitment and considerable cost. Not a decision that should be made on behalf of someone else.

I found Max a great home with a family who had lost their terrier to old age and were ready to get another dog. With experienced owners, reward-based training, consistent handling and regular exercise, Max was transformed from a fearful, stressed dog, into a loving family companion.

Notes to self:
Don't mess with elderly ladies bearing walking sticks.

Pole Dancing

Lex was a beautiful three-year-old St. Bernard who, despite his huge size, was a gentle giant and a real sweetheart. He sported a red spotted bandana that, whilst adding a touch of the debonair, also served the practical purpose of absorbing some of the copious amount of slobber he produced. When he shook himself, strings of saliva wrapped around his head in a slimy bonnet, while projectile globules of goo flew out in all directions. If you were unlucky enough to be in range, you had best have a good supply of tissues. St. Bernards, lovely dogs, but they could do with an 'off' tap.

His owner, Tomasz, was Polish and a large man with an easy smile and a relaxed nature. I had previously given a basic training lesson at his home. Tomasz and

Lex had been quick learners and had progressed well. Tomasz felt that it would be beneficial to have a lead training lesson out on location at his local town park, so we made arrangements to meet up.

It was a Saturday and despite the light rain, there were a number of people out and about. There were other dog walkers in the park as well as a few children wrapped up against the weather, playing on the swings. I wanted a quiet area to work, so we made our way past the playing fields, where a group of muddy lads were playing a raucous game of five-a-side football and headed towards the far side of the park.

There we took a tree-lined path that sloped steeply upwards and as we made the steady climb, I began to experience muscle spasms in my lower back. This is a recurring issue. By the time we reached the summit, my usual long-legged stride was reduced to the tiny steps of a geisha girl. What I really needed was an anti-inflammatory, a hot bath and a lie down. This not being an option, I settled for stopping for a while.

Often when out lead training, I utilise objects for marking out a distance for elliptical circuits and figure-of-eight lead work. There just happened to be a handy signpost pole and a nearby lamppost for this purpose. This allowed me to lean against the pole to rest my back, while I set Tomasz and Lex to work on a right-hand circuit. I watched them move towards and away from me as they circled the markers, giving instructions to stop and execute some basic commands before changing direction.

Tomasz was working Lex on an extendable lead that was locked short. I prefer to use a standard nylon lead for heel work but he suffered from arthritis in his hands and found the large handle easier to manage. They were doing well and Tomasz was looking very pleased with himself when suddenly, he tripped. Stumbling and trying to right himself, Tomasz landed heavily on top of Lex's paw. Unfortunately, this occurred just as they approached the post I was leaning against. In pain and surprise, Lex jumped sideways just as Tomasz accidentally knocked the lock off the lead which allowed him to take off on its full eight metre length.

He ran past the post and then circled back, running around in circles in a panic, the lead reeling out in thigh-high coils that encompassed the pole, myself and Tomasz. With my back the way it was, I was unable to extract myself from the resulting tangle. When Lex had reached his third circuit, Tomasz hit the brake on the lead, which, given the dog's weight and momentum, resulted in the tightening of the whole thing. I was now tied to a pole, face-to-face with a middle-aged man I hardly knew, with 120kg of Saint Bernard still straining on the lead, pinning us tightly in place. Lex was panting and drooling, Tomasz was grinning enthusiastically and

I was thinking, *Oh God, let that be a dog toy in his pocket!*

If this wasn't bad enough, the sign on the post we were tied to proclaimed, 'Dogs must be kept on leads.'

Oh the irony.

Our predicament was witnessed by a couple who stopped to watch with no small amount of amusement. I am eternally grateful that neither one had a video camera; I could imagine that footage going viral on YouTube.

Notes to self:

Posts and extendable leads — in close proximity — should be avoided at all costs.

The Human Kite

Sometimes when I am out and about, I see people with dogs who would benefit from some professional help. Dogs that have had no lead training, gagging and choking on a choke chain while dragging their owners down the road. Owners on the beach who have let their dogs off the lead, but omitted to train them to come back. With the dog running around out of control they attempt to catch it, getting more and more frustrated and angry. This doesn't usually bode well for the dog when they do finally manage to grab them.

I have seen owners in some predicaments, but this one took the ticket.

Just on the outskirts of town there is a river walk that is popular with dog owners. The river banks are steep and in between thickets of brambles are paths worn by many feet, giving access down to the water's edge. Reed beds supply a haven for wildlife and nesting birds with frequent sightings of ducks, geese and pairs of majestic swans. The walkway that runs along the river has a drainage ditch with a thick hedgerow on the other side, making the path narrow and separating it from a sizable piece of bog land.

When working with owners I sometimes enlisted the help of my dear departed German Shepherd. I rescued Woulfe when he was a year old from an owner who used to beat him with a chain. He had mange, which had been neglected and his bald skin was covered in weeping lesions. Between the physical neglect and psychological damage he needed a lot of TLC. He blossomed into the most wonderful companion and working partner. He was exceptional.

We had been out on a training session, and as a reward I had decided to take Woulfe down to the river before heading home. Working our way along the path we were playing games with his toys, when I noticed a Red Setter a little distance away, heading towards us.

Setters only have two speed settings: stop, or go. They are bred for hunting partridge and grouse, and while casting for a scent, they can cover incredible distances, working at high speed, and with total focus and intensity. Once they have pinned down the location of prey, they freeze to indicate where they are.

This dog had all the right instincts; he was enthusiastically casting for a scent, but was being rather hampered by the annoying weight on the other end of the lead. Nose in the air, he was attempting to run with the human kite getting yanked from right to left, the young woman was struggling to remain upright as she was getting pulled off her feet. Her shouts of, 'JAKE, NNOOO, JAKE, STOP, JAKE, WILL YOU BEHAVE,' carried to us on the wind.

I could hardly bring myself to watch as the Setter suddenly dived to the right, taking off down the slope towards the river. Luckily, just at that point, there was a bench that the lady grabbed hold of, and so managed to prevent being dragged down into the water.

Phew! That was close.

At this point obviously deciding that enough was enough, with much pulling and tugging she managed to turn the dog and they retraced their lurching steps back the way they had just come. I thought, as we followed a little distance behind, that I really should give her one of my business cards, when the dog caught an interesting scent from the neighbouring field. He leaped sideways away from the river, pulling the lady completely off her feet and dragging her into the drainage gully on the other side. She was trying to right herself, slipping and sliding in the muddy water when the dog squeezed through a small gap in the bottom of the hedgerow pulling her along with him.

She started shouting and screaming as she was getting dragged through the hedge, her hair and jacket getting snagged on the branches. Fair play to her, she didn't want to relinquish the lead, but inevitably had to let go. Jake took off into the neighbouring field and she fell back into the muddy ditch water.

The poor lady was quite shaken up. Covered in scratches, her clothes were torn, muddy and soaked with brackish water, the term 'she looked like she had been dragged through a hedge backwards' couldn't have been more apt. Giving her a hand out of the trench, she looked about to burst into tears.

Collapsing onto the grass, pulling twigs from her hair, she explained that it was her sister's dog and she was afraid that she wouldn't be able to get him back, which was why she had been slow to let go of the lead.

Looking through the hedgerow, I could see the Setter bouncing around the boggy field like a spring lamb, muddy water spraying up at every turn thoroughly enjoying himself. Apparently Jake was very sociable with other dogs, so there was only one thing I could do; I sent Woulfe in to bring him back. My dear Woulfe, always dependable, he crawled through the gap and went about rounding him up. A short time later Jake came back through another break in the hedging a little further up the path, with Woulfe right behind him, both dogs totally plastered in mud. Between effective herding from Woulfe and my enthusiastic encouragement we were successful.

I walked Jake back to the lady's car as she was in no state to manage. She was visiting her sister and had felt sorry for Jake as he was never walked, so she had decided to give him a treat by taking him down to the river.

I gave her my number in case her sister wanted some help with training, but never did hear from her.

I lost Woulfe to cancer when he was nine years old, it broke my heart. I still feel his loss deeply to this day. Loyal and true, run free my beautiful Woulfe.

Lessons learnt:
You can't squeeze a human-sized body through a dog-sized hole.

Changing Perceptions

Often, training and behaviour problems in dogs are caused by the attitude and actions of the owner. Dog behaviourists do not just work with dogs, we also have to modify the owner's perception and change their behaviour as well.

Sandra phoned me about her boyfriend's dog, which she described as the dog from hell, citing a considerably long list of complaints about his antics. Apparently they had two dogs; her own dog Millie was extremely well behaved, but Jack needed some serious work. We arranged an appointment for Sandra, Michael and Jack to visit my office.

When they arrived, Sandra was out of the car first, she was very brusque in her manner, brushing dog hair from her black pencil skirt before striding in, her blonde hair pulled tightly back from her pinched features. Her body language was stiff and in order to shake my proffered hand she had to uncurl her fists. There was a lot of anger boiling just beneath the surface. Inviting her to take a seat, I watched Michael reluctantly get out of the car. In contrast he was casually dressed in jeans and a T-shirt. Retrieving a small worried-looking Jack Russell from the back seat, he shuffled in looking like a man who wished he were somewhere else. When he sat next to Sandra, she crossed her arms and legs and turned her back towards him. The couple didn't seem to be on talking terms and I had the impression that a blazing row had occurred on the way over.

Jack was hiding behind Michael's legs looking very unsure. Putting a few treats in a feeding toy, I put it just far enough away from him to encourage him out from under the chair. Piquing his interest, he came out to investigate. He snuffled up the loose treats that had fallen out of the toy, before beginning to focus on working out how to get to the rest. I commented on what a nice little dog he was, which brought a snort of derision from Sandra. Hoping that allowing her to express her grievances might help to alleviate some of the tension, I invited her to begin. It was obvious from the outset that she really didn't like Jack, he could do no right and she had a list of complaints.

Jack is the dog from hell, whilst Millie is an angel

because she has trained her.

Jack's total disobedience is because *he* — jerking her thumb at Michael — hasn't trained him, whereas Millie is the model canine citizen.

Jack jumps up on the furniture when he knows he is not allowed, and *he* — looking daggers at Michael — positively encourages him. *Her* dog never gets on the furniture.

Jack is not allowed on the bed, but every time Sandra goes out she comes home to find dog hairs on the bed even though Michael denies that he has let him up there. Michael lies!

Millie sits quietly by her feet in the evening, while Jack constantly runs around barking and jumping on and off the furniture. Sandra gets a rolled up newspaper to punish him, but she can never catch him as he runs round and around the table. The dog has no discipline whatsoever.

Millie is very good on the lead, Jack is a nightmare. He pulls, barks, lunges at people and is a total embarrassment, again, because he has not been trained. More dirty looks in Michael's direction.

During her tirade, Michael sat quietly, occasionally shaking his head. Jack had emptied the toy, and while listening to Sandra, I encouraged him over and got him to sit using a treat as a lure. I only had to do it twice. He learnt very quickly that if he came over to me and sat, he got a reward. He was such a nice dog and so quick to learn, I felt really sorry for him, with Michael coming in a close second in the sympathy stakes.

By the time Sandra got all this off her chest, her body language was beginning to unwind. I began to take a detailed history, concentrating specifically on asking Michael questions to try and bring him out a little and express his views. Once I had some information, I began to ask questions that required the couple to collaborate on the answers, which helped to open up the lines of communication between them. We were now in a position to start resolving the issues.

Sandra was working under the assumption that Jack was being naughty just to wind her up. Once in possession of the facts, I was able to present an explanation of the situation from Jack's perspective. When he lived alone with Michael they had their own routine, he had spent most evenings on Michael's lap on the couch and also slept with him on his bed. Suddenly Jack's world was turned upside down. Sandra and Millie moved in, bringing about major changes, Michael had moved to a new job with longer working hours. Behaviour that was previously acceptable suddenly resulted in unpredictable and frightening behaviour from Sandra, while still being actively encouraged by Michael. Jack was totally confused and suffering from stress, causing hyperactivity and excessive barking.

Sandra's reaction was to shout and try to hit him with a rolled up newspaper, which further aggravated the situation.

Once Sandra considered the situation from the dog's point of view, her attitude towards Jack began to soften. The next step was to help them build a more positive relationship, so that Sandra would begin to see what great potential Jack had if she gave him the opportunity. By encouraging Sandra to use positive reinforcement training it would change their relationship from a negative one to a positive one.

We soon had Jack sitting, lying down and hand touching on command. He was a little star. Sandra couldn't believe how easy he was to train with the right approach; I have never seen such an immediate and total change of opinion. She was smiling and couldn't praise Jack enough. She was so pleased that I had to insist that Michael have a chance to practise as well, otherwise she would have taken over the whole process. Seemingly Michael was still in the dog house.

The next thing on the agenda was to get some compromise and agreement on consistent house rules for Jack. After some negotiating they both agreed that Jack was definitely not allowed on the bed, but he would be allowed on the couch and they both promised to abide by the rules.

We then took Jack out to start lead training. He

responded admirably, and within ten minutes he was walking like the model dog. He was a dream to work with, so responsive and eager to please. Sandra was absolutely delighted with this and was not inclined to let Michael take his turn with the lead, without my insistence.

I phoned Sandra a few days later for a progress report; she was amazed by the improvement and said it was like someone had swapped Jack for a different dog. The truth was that he always had been a great little dog; in this case, it was the owner's behaviour that needed modification. Sandra said she now had a better relationship with Jack, than she did with her own dog and when they went out for a walk, she insisted that Michael take Millie while she took Jack. I suggested that she spend some quality time with Millie, and apply the same positive training techniques.

I often wonder if Sandra and Michael are still together, and if they did part company, who took custody of Michael's dog.

Lessons Learnt:
Behaviour modification can be challenging when applied to humans.

The Velcro Cat

Dogs I understand, cats, not so much. While I like and admire them, they are a complete enigma to me. Our family cat has us all trained with impressive efficiency. Daisy, or as she is affectionately known in our house as 'she who must be obeyed', keeps the entire family busy with her constant and insistent requests. Having lost a hind leg to a road traffic accident, she is not able to jump very well. If she is not demanding to be lifted up for food, she is asking to be let down because she has finished eating. There are also the constant requests to scratch her ear. She purrs, pressing against your hand while her little leg stump goes through all the motions of ghost scratching. Without warning, she decides she has had enough and lets you have it, turning on you with teeth and claws. This cat actually sits by the litter tray, complaining, because she wants a clean tray to poo in!

Dogs have owners, cats have staff; so true.

The problem with cats is that they are armed with an arsenal of sharp pointy things and they know how to use them to good effect. With their Jekyll and Hyde personalities, unpredictable behaviour and 'take no prisoners' attitude they can be quite formidable. This was evident in an incident at one of the local vets.

I work closely with vets and rescue groups and sometimes do voluntary training and behavioural work with dogs to help improve their chances of re-homing. A dog had been brought into one of the vets to be put to sleep as the owner was unable to cope due to health problems. The dog was young and healthy so the vet persuaded the owner into handing the dog over to get a new home. He had then asked me to call in and do some work with him.

When I arrived, the vet was busy with a client. Being on familiar terms with the staff, Ann, one of the vet nurses, took me through the prep room and into the kennel area to meet the dog in question. Suddenly, a door burst open and hit against the wall, and I heard the vet's voice getting louder as he approached muttering some choice expletives.

As we peered around the corner to see what was going on, we saw the vet. He stood shoulders hunched, his empty arms standing out from his body. He was muttering away to himself, looking down at a cat firmly attached where no cat ought to be. She had clamped her teeth into the flesh just below his navel and further secured her position by wrapping all four legs around his upper thigh. Her left front claws were firmly hooked into one buttock, and the other front leg disappeared between his legs.

I found out later that it had happened just after the vet had given her an injection to sedate her. The cat had panicked, shot off the table and clamped onto the vet with all five weapons. The sedation, which unfortunately hadn't taken full effect, caused the cat to freeze into position.

It was a situation that you know you shouldn't find funny, but you just can't help yourself. Ann let out an involuntary snort of laughter. I gave up trying to control my face and instead concentrated on trying to prevent the impending belly laugh from escaping. Hearing us chortle, the vet looked up with a sheepish grin asking if we could lend a hand.

The cat was stuck on like Velcro, and it took all three of us to carefully peel her off. This was a tricky operation given the location of said cat. Myself and Ann were trying to help as best we could without getting too close to any sensitive areas of the vet, which only added to the hilarity.

Notes to self:

Stick to working with dogs.

Lessons learnt:

It takes at least three people to extract a vet from a semi-conscious cat.

Shocking

In some respects I can be quite tough. I have to treat aggressive dogs of all sizes, which is not for the faint hearted, particularly when dealing with giant breeds. I once went around in considerable pain thinking I had pulled a muscle doing yoga. After a month I thought perhaps I should go to the doctor as it seemed to be going on a bit, only to discover I had two broken ribs. I have gone through childbirth twice without any difficulty. However, there are two things in life that turn me into a lily-livered scaredy-cat.

My biggest fear is electricity, it absolutely terrifies me. I even get freaked out by the static discharge you sometimes get from shopping trolleys at the supermarket. This phobia of mine sprang into existence when I was a child and involved a squeezy bottle full of water, an exploding light bulb and a bath full of glass, but that's another story. I mention this by way of an explanation for my ineffectual behaviour in the following incident.

As a side note, the other things that I dislike intensely are clowns. They are creepy and disturbing, but fortunately have no involvement here.

I count myself lucky to live in a detached cottage in rural Ireland. Our property is surrounded on all sides by grazing fields; in summer it is not unusual to wake up to see cows peering in the bedroom from the boundary six feet away. When the fields are unoccupied, our neighbour allows us to use his land for our dogs. It is sizable and is divided up into three fields, each separated by a three-foot high, single wire electric fence. In order to cross from one field to another, it is necessary to duck underneath the live fence. Not being particularly limber and experiencing a heart pounding fear of getting a shock, I always execute this manoeuvre with extreme care. I have to nearly prostrate myself on the grass and roll underneath, making sure there is a good two-foot distance between me and the wire.

On this particular day, I was taking four of my more energetic dogs down to the river at the end of the field, the best access point being one field over. Most of our dogs go under the fence, with the exception of our dear departed Collie Cross. Conan, an absolute character, liked to use the fence for agility practise. Ears up, tongue lolling and looking highly delighted with himself he would spring back and forth jumping over it several times, just because he could.

He had already cleared the fence twice but on the next attempt totally misjudged the take-off making him land short. He ended up across the fence, his front feet on the ground and his back legs hooked over the wire. He was stuck. To make matters worse, the wire was passing over the most sensitive part of his anatomy.

These fences are designed to keep cattle in, so have a high level of voltage which pulses through the wire at regular intervals. I didn't have to guess how frequently this occurred, as Conan let out a yelp each time he got a shock, which gave me a very good indication. I really wanted to help him off but I knew that if I touched him as the current was passing through, I would get a shock as well. I broke into a sweat, my arms braced to intervene trying to pin down the timing. I was actually making whimpering sounds as I started several attempts, only to chicken out at the last moment. It really was pathetic. Eventually love conquered fear, but my poor dog got at least five hits before I plucked up the courage to lift him off.

That was the last time Conan ever tried to jump the fence.

Lessons learnt:

Overcoming a phobia is possible given the right incentive: eventually. Sorry Conan!

Jack Russell Surprise

Dogs enrich our lives in so many ways. With their intelligence, loyalty and companionship, it is sometimes easy to forget that although highly domesticated, they are still predators. We like to think that our own pets are incapable of causing harm, but aggression is a normal component of canine behaviour and any dog given the right set of circumstances can be capable of inflicting serious injuries.

When treating cases of aggression the safety of all concerned is the priority. Risks can be minimised, however, with correct handling and management, but even us professionals get caught out occasionally and sometimes in the most unexpected ways.

Declan had been referred to me by one of the vets. His two-year-old Jack Russell Terrier, Snapper — not the most encouraging name — was aggressive with dogs, hated children and had bitten several visitors to his home. His last victim had wanted him put to sleep but had agreed to a stay of execution to allow Declan to get professional advice. We spoke at length on the telephone and I stressed the importance of preventing any further incidents, giving detailed instructions on how to introduce Snapper to a muzzle in a positive way so he would be quite happy to wear it. We made arrangements for a house call for the following week.

Declan lived in one of the housing estates in town which has a certain reputation. After navigating over multiple speed bumps, around a burnt-out car and the odd abandoned shopping trolley, I finally managed to find his house. Tucked away in the corner of a cul-de-sac, the unhinged rusty gate led onto a small unkempt garden. Rusty paint cans and various other detritus protruded above the weeds. As I made my way up the overgrown path, Declan opened the door and ushered me into a cramped hallway. Stacks of newspapers and boxes piled along one side took up half of the floor space. A pungent aroma of stale urine and boiled cabbage hung in the air. Taking care not to disturb the precarious piles, I followed Declan down to a door at the end of the hall. This led into a small kitchen/diner. The room was divided into two by an island of kitchen units and Snapper was in a cramped space between this and an armchair. He was wearing a basket muzzle and was licking his lips and growling, the whites of his eyes clearly showing as he alternated between cowering away from me and lunging at my boots. He was extremely fearful, and the tight quarters were further aggravating the problem, making him feel trapped. Amongst the furniture and clutter, the majority of the remaining floor space was taken up with a round table swathed in a stained cloth that draped to the floor. Emanating from the depths beneath could be heard the occasional rumblings of an unseen dog. Declan explained that Betsy, who was Snapper's mother had her bed under there, and not to pay any attention to her as she wasn't any trouble.

I felt Snapper would cope better in a more open environment, so Declan put him on an extendable lead and we took him out to the back garden. Despite the piles of scrap metal and lumber it was a large garden, with a good size area free of clutter. Although still nervous, Snapper was less fearful with more room to move. He was circling, watching me intently but keeping his distance. While observing his behaviour, I began to question Declan about his history. I had asked the owner not to pay any attention to Snapper and as we talked he gradually became less focused on me and more interested in the environment.

Ten minutes into the session and Snapper was

57

beginning to gain a little confidence, tentatively moving closer to investigate my scent. Being careful not to move and startle him, I carried on talking to Declan. At that point, someone in the house opened the back door and let Betsy out. She went off down the garden and didn't seem to be taking any notice of us so I turned my attention back to the job in hand. Declan was just filling me in on details of the most recent incident, when without warning a weight slammed into me from behind and I felt a sharp pain in the top of my thigh. *What the…*

Looking over my shoulder I saw Betsy. She was swinging like a pendulum, all four feet off the ground, trying to tear a bite-sized piece out of my pants. There was the inevitable ripping sound as she dropped to the ground with a chunk of blood-splattered material in her jaws. After giving it a good shake, she spat it out before running around to face me and launching herself towards me, biting me on the shin. *Ooh, you little…* Declan managed to grab Betsy just as she was jumping in for a third bite. So much for her not being any trouble.

Declan finally admitted that Betsy had in fact bitten quite a few people, and two of her other offspring who had been homed to friends, had been put to sleep for aggression. Facts he had omitted to tell me when I had asked him specifically about any family history of aggression. He had been afraid to mention it, as he thought that I would recommend immediate euthanasia for both Betsy and Snapper and he didn't want to lose his dogs. Had he been honest from the outset, it would have saved a perfectly good pair of pants.

You cannot always cure aggression, but this does not necessarily mean that the dog has to be destroyed. With strict management you can prevent further incidents from occurring and with behaviour modification you can gain some improvement. This necessitates total commitment from the owner and, fair play to Declan, he agreed to additional sessions and followed instructions to the letter. While both dogs would always need to be muzzled for safety when around people, with hard work and dedication on Declan's part, both dogs improved.

I still check in with Declan from time to time and the last time we spoke, he reported that Snapper was more confident with people and was much improved. Sadly, Betsy had passed away finally giving in to old age. She had died in her bed under the table. RIP Betsy.

Over the years, particularly when working as a veterinary assistant, I have been on the receiving end of numerous bites. It is a bit ironic that the only bite to date while treating aggression was not from the dog which was under treatment. But perhaps I shouldn't speak too soon...

Notes to self:

Buy thicker pants.

Things that make you go . . . Hmmm

Over the years, I have worked with countless owners, the vast majority of whom have been a pleasure to teach. Unfortunately in this profession you also have to deal with more than a few time wasters and people with unreasonable expectations. There are also those that expect you to make yourself available at all times of day and night to facilitate their needs.

I was once woken at 2 a.m. by the phone ringing. At that late hour, I thought that it might be a family emergency. Groggy with sleep, I forced myself out of bed and with trepidation I answered the call. I could barely interpret the slurred voice on the other end of the phone and I was beginning to worry that it was someone who had suffered a stroke or was in serious need of an ambulance. Eventually I realised that in fact it was an extremely drunk chap who wanted to know if I could help him train his dog.

Given his level of his intoxication I doubt that he was able to remember how rude I was.

On another occasion I had someone knocking on my door at 11 p.m. on a Sunday night, setting off all my dogs and waking the children when they had school in the morning. When I opened the door, a man was standing there holding a puppy in his arms. He expected me to take it in for a few weeks for house training.

I wasn't very polite on that occasion either.

Sometimes people want me to take their dogs away and bring them back perfectly trained. They generally fall into two types. Too posh to train; these are usually people with delusions of grandeur because they have a little woman who 'does' a couple of times a week. They consider the training of the dog as something that the staff should handle. Then there are the people who are just lazy. These people just don't want to be bothered investing any time in their dogs. What is the point of having a dog, if you do not want to spend time with them? My job is to teach owners how to train their own dogs, which is a fundamental component in the development of their relationship and the only way to achieve lasting success. I do not do 'take it away and train it'.

Another frequent scenario involves phone calls

from people who expect me to come round to stop their dog from barking constantly, pulling washing off the line and digging up the plants. Invariably, the dog lives in the back garden, has never been taken for a walk and has no stimulation or company. The only time they see anyone is in the morning when someone puts their food out. Patiently I explain to them that the first step to resolving these issues will involve them giving the dog a life. This is not usually what they want to hear because it takes some effort on their part, they would much prefer not to get involved and just arrange for me to pop round with my magic wand and super human powers and fix it.

To be a successful dog trainer you need a lot of patience, which fortunately I have in spades; on the whole I have a calm and tolerant personality. There was one incident, however, that challenged even my incredibly long fuse.

I was late home and exhausted after a long drive down to the south coast of Kerry on a behaviour case. I had just grabbed a bite to eat and was getting ready to hit the shower before going to bed when the phone rang. I was half expecting a phone call from my brother, so I picked it up.

It was a woman's voice. 'Is that the lady who trains the dogs?'

I sighed. It was 9.30 p.m. and I wasn't particularly in the mood. 'Yes, but it is a little late, could you call me tomorrow?'

'I have a serious problem; I might have to put my dog down. I just need a few minutes of your time,' she stated.

My shower was going to have to wait. 'Right, what's the problem?'

'I have a Great Dane, and he keeps chasing people up the road and attacking them. He's knocked two children off their bikes and last week he actually bit a teenager who was trying to fend him off.' She went on to explain that he had also attacked several dogs which were passing by. She was now getting complaints from her neighbours, who were threatening to phone the dog warden. Her husband was considerably put out that they had been required to pay both veterinary and doctor's bills for the victims.

The immediate issue was not one of training, rather the need for the owners to start taking their responsibilities seriously. My first question was the obvious one. 'Why are you allowing this to happen?'

'I am not sure what you mean,' she said. 'I am phoning because I want *you* to come round and train him not to go out in the road and attack people.'

Oh you do, do you? If I was a dog it would have been at this point that my hackles would have started to rise.

'Tell me,' I said, 'how is he getting off your

property?'

'It's only at the entrance where he gets out; the rest of the garden has high stone walls.'

'Well surely then,' I said, 'it would be easy enough to put up gates.'

'Oh we already have six foot iron gates,' she says.

'Then how is he getting out, is he squeezing through the bars or what?'

Her answer stopped me in my tracks. 'Oh no, he can only get out when we leave them open.'

The last vestiges of my patience blew away like smoke on the wind. I am pretty sure that my lips curled back over my teeth as I growled, 'And why are you leaving them open?'

'Well,' she says. 'It's just that it is very inconvenient for us to have to keep getting in and out of the car, opening and shutting them so we leave them open all the time; it's just laziness really.'

That was the final straw. The end of my fuse was well and truly reached and the explosion at the end of it ignited, blowing professionalism and tact out the window. These owners were responsible for causing physical injuries to passers-by and possibly long-term psychological damage as well. I have worked with people who have developed cynophobia — a fear of dogs — after experiencing this type of incident. It can be life changing and can affect their overall confidence.

Children are particularly vulnerable.

Other dogs had also received injuries that required veterinary attention and they were putting their own dog in danger of destruction. Not to mention the risk of causing a road accident. All because they were too lazy to shut the gate. I couldn't comprehend that they had allowed so many instances to occur when it was so easily prevented.

I spent the next several minutes reading her the riot act and telling her in no uncertain terms exactly what I thought of her irresponsible behaviour. The outcome was her solemn promise to make sure the gate was kept shut at all times, and a commitment to a few training and behaviour sessions, which yielded positive results.

Notes to self:

Patience is a virtue.

Impeccably Trained Owner Awards

People routinely underestimate the intelligence of dogs. I have often heard owners complaining that their dog is un-trainable, because s/he is stupid. On the contrary, although the owner has most certainly failed to train the dog, invariably the dog has the humans jumping through hoops. They can be so subtle about this process that the owners do not even realise how well trained they have become.

Over the years I have met some dogs who proved to be efficient people trainers and feel they ought to get some recognition for their hard work and perseverance.

Following tradition, The Impeccably Trained Owner Awards are presented in reverse order:

In third place - Ben the Shih Tzu.

Ben discovered that if he barked when his owner went near the fridge, he would get cheese. He developed a bit of a taste for it, so began to concentrate his efforts on the lady of the house who was the main hunter/gatherer. After diligent hard work he managed to secure his very own supply of his favourite vintage cheddar. This was known as 'Ben's cheese' and was not for anyone else. By refusing to eat his dog food he began to train his owner to sprinkle extra grated cheese on top, gradually shaping her behaviour until every meal contained cheese. The good thing about humans is that you only have to teach one and they will pass on the training to the rest. Ingenious. Eventually Ben had the whole family trained to give him cheese on demand. Nicely done, Ben!

In second place - Fritz the Norwegian Elkhound.

Fritz realised that if he was slow to eat his dinner, his owner would hand feed him. He rather enjoyed this quality time with his owner so he diligently worked on this until he had her trained to feed him his entire dinner, one nut at a time. Fritz didn't stop there however; he developed this further until he would only accept the proffered dinner while enjoying the comfort of his arm chair. The lady had to get up extra early for work, as it took around twenty minutes to feed him. I particularly admired the fact that when Fritz was fed, the owner perched on a hard kitchen chair, while Fritz got the comfortable option. Good effort, Fritz!

A well-deserved first prize - Bob the West Highland Terrier.

Bob trained his owner, Diana, to constantly throw toys for the entire duration of Coronation Street, which happened to be her favourite TV programme. He discovered this almost by accident one evening. All he needed to do to initiate the game was to throw his ball at Diana's feet and start barking. Diana's response was to throw his toy to shut him up so she could hear the show. Bob soon learnt that when he heard the Coronation Street theme tune, it was time to find his ball. His retrieve was so fast that I worked out that Diana must throw his toy at least ninety times during a thirty minute programme. Brilliant, well done, Bob!

And Finally

I hope you have enjoyed reading about some of my adventures as much as I have enjoyed writing about them.

I am delighted to announce that Bob the Westie has agreed to collaborate with me on a book for his fellow canines. 'Bob's Guide to Training Humans', all the tips and tricks from the master.

For all the latest news on up and coming publications, canine health articles, great photos and general doggie stuff join me on Facebook!

https://www.facebook.com/SmartdogBooks

Other Publications

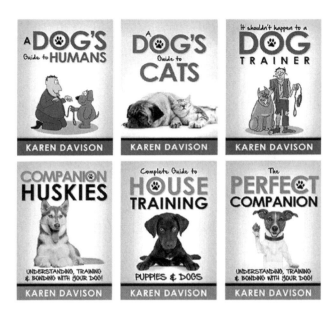

FUN READS FOR DOG LOVERS SERIES

A Dog's Guide to Humans

Have you ever wondered how dogs see us?

A lighthearted look at the human species from a dog's point of view. Bob the West Highland Terrier shares some tips and tricks on getting the best out of human beings, attempts to fathom some of their strange behaviour and imparts some of his wisdom on training and manipulation techniques.

A must have book for all canines!

Is YOUR dog a master human trainer?

Take the quiz at the end of the book to find out!

A Dog's Guide to Cats

Bob the Westie once again puts paw to paper to offer a few pearls of wisdom to his fellow canines. This time it's the old enemy… Cats.

Don't be fooled by their apparent small stature and fluffy cuteness, these things have super powers that you can only dream of, and their instincts are as sharp as their claws. Luckily help is at hand

A Dog's Guide to Cats contains all dogs need to get one step ahead of the game, including how to build a cunning trap that will give hours of cat free pleasure!

Packed with vital information, it also includes some heart wrenching and cautionary tales sent in by fellow canines.

Can Bob help them find solutions to their cat problems?

POSITIVE DOG TRAINING SERIES

The Perfect Companion
Understanding, Training and Bonding with your Dog!

This book explores the inner workings of the dog's mind to give you a real understanding of how and why, positive reinforcement gains the best and most reliable results.

You will find detailed instructions on how to teach all the basic commands, using various different positive training techniques, so that you can choose the method that best suits you and your dog.

It encourages you to consider your dog's natural behaviour and to channel their instincts into positive activities, and reveals why stimulating your dog's mind, has many behavioural and physical benefits, possibly contributing to longevity. Environmental enrichment and suggested activities and games, will not only give your dog a confident, happy and fulfilled life, it will also strengthen the bond between you, taking your relationship to a whole new level.

Some common behavioural issues are covered in detail, explaining the causes, prevention and solutions, as well as a general problem solving guide, with a checklist to help you diagnose the root cause of problems, and suggests what action may be needed, in order to resolve them.

The Perfect Companion, Understanding, Training and Bonding with your Dog! Written by professional dog trainer and canine behaviourist, Karen Davison, is essential reading for all new puppy owners, and a valuable source of information for those of us, who want to get the best out of our relationship with man's best friend

Complete Guide to Housetraining
Puppies and Dogs

Do you need advice on housebreaking? This guide will give you the means to success!

Take the stress out of housetraining and get positive results - fast. A must have guide for teaching your puppy or dog to be clean in the house. With the right approach, house training can be reasonably quick and easy. This guide shows you how.

Topics covered:- Positive approach, effective clean up regimes, first steps to success, training methods, teaching your dog to go on command, diet and nutrition, advantages and disadvantages of neutering, crate training, common mistakes, dos and don'ts.

Companion Huskies
Understanding, Training and Bonding with your Dog!

Combines The Perfect Companion and Housetraining Puppies and Dogs, this book is adapted specifically for this high energy breed and explores all aspects of husky ownership from puppyhood to maturity.

Bonus items, breed information, hereditary disorders, socialisation program and husky sports.

About the
Author

Karen Davison grew up in Bedfordshire, England. She has been both an avid reader and a lover of animals since early childhood. When she was eight, the family got their first dog, Scamp, whose great character started Karen's lifelong devotion to dogs.

Since qualifying in Canine Psychology in 2001, she has worked as a professional dog trainer and canine behaviourist. She went on to study Wolf Ecology in 2009 and was lucky enough to spend time with the wolves at the UK Wolf Conservation Trust in Reading.

Her first publication, The Perfect Companion: Understanding, Training and Bonding with your Dog, a comprehensive guide to canine psychology, training and problem solving, was published in June 2012 and won an IndiePENdants' award for quality. Since then she has published The Complete Guide to House Training Puppies and Dogs, Companion Huskies: Understanding, Training and Bonding with your Dog, and three Fun Reads for Dog Lovers: A

Dog's Guide to Humans, A Dog's Guide to Cats and It Shouldn't Happen to a Dog Trainer.

After joining a local writers group, she has spread her author wings and is now enjoying writing poetry, flash fiction and short stories, and after taking a course in screenwriting has just completed her first radio drama script. She is currently working on her first work of fiction, which combines her love of writing, wolves and fantasy - Wolf Clan Rising which is due to be published 2017, under pen name K.D. Phelan.. You can find an excerpt of Wolf Clan Rising at the end of this publication.

Karen is now living the dream, she resides in a country cottage on the west coast of Ireland, drawing inspiration for her writing from the peace and beauty of her surroundings where she shares her life with her husband, two daughters and nine special needs pets. Her seven rescue dogs and two rescue cats have a mixture of emotional, behavioural and physical disabilities

One of Karen's favourite sayings: 'Saving one dog will not change the world, but surely for that one dog, the world will change forever.'

Meet the author, join Karen on Facebook:-
https://www.facebook.com/SmartdogBooks

WOLF CLAN RISING

Book One

K.D. PHELAN

For generations, men and wolves have formed an alliance. Companions and hunting partners, the clan and the pack have formed a special bond, but it is breeding season and wolves are free spirits.

Despite being surrounded by family and friends, Andrik feels alone. His wolf has gone, to return in summer with a new mate and offspring to strengthen the bloodlines. To Andrik, summer seems an age away.

The mage's dreams are haunted by a dark spirit. It moves through the forest, its limbs, tentacle like and writhing, turn everything to ash.

It is a warning, but what does it mean?

Laya knows, she has seen it in a dream that is not a dream. There are strangers in the forest... and they are hunting wolves. A boy travels with them, born into slavery in a city far across the ocean, he had never questioned his fate, but the forest has stirred something deep inside him. Will he have the courage to betray his masters to save the wolf?

The invaders won't stop until they have stripped the land and enslaved its people. With the help of magic can the clans prevail? Or is this the beginning of the end for the hunter-gatherers?

Excerpt from Wolf Clan Rising.

Chapter One
BLEYD

The setting sun filters through the forest, casting golden rays that dance with the spirits of the living canopy. Through the dappled sunlight, a lone wolf moves on silent paws along the narrow trail, his powerful legs cover the ground at an easy trot.

Far to the north, the distant howls of stranger wolves carry to him faintly on the wind; he pauses, pricking his ears towards the sound. Licking his nose he inhales to explore his surroundings.

The north east wind brings with it the scent of snow from the high peaks and the freshness of the White Water river. Close by, rain and earth, the souls of trees, and spirits of a myriad living things that inhabit the forest. The wolf smells what is and also, what has gone before. The older scents are fainter, like the tracks of ghosts.

He registers this in a few heartbeats then lifts his muzzle and flaring his nostrils, casts his mind out further still, seeking the one scent that has caused such restlessness. The one that surrounds him, an invisible force that pulls him further and further away from his pack.

The scent of the she-wolf.

On the wind, a minute trace of what he seeks causes his heart to race. He lifts his head and raw emotion flows from his lips, quietly at first, rising and falling until the air is filled with a long and wavering howl. Caught by the wind, it travels through the forest.

Away to the south his own pack add their song, their voices weaving around his, wrapping him with warmth and comfort, and bringing with it an overwhelming sense of loss.

In the midst of the voices, he hears his soul brother calling to him. His chest tightens and for a moment he looks back over his shoulder but as twilight descends, the faint cry of the she-wolf beckons him north.

Printed in Great Britain
by Amazon